THE AMERICAN POETRY REVIEW/HONICKMAN FIRST BOOK PRIZE

The Honickman Foundation is dedicated to the support of projects that promote spiritual growth and creativity, education and social change. At the heart of the mission of the Honickman Foundation is the belief that creativity enriches contemporary society because the arts are powerful tools for enlightenment, equity and empowerment, and must be encouraged to effect social change as well as personal growth. A current focus is on the particular power of photography and poetry to reflect and interpret reality, and, hence, to illuminate all that is true.

The annual American Poetry Review/Honickman First Book Prize offers publication of a book of poems, a $3,000 award, and distribution by Copper Canyon Press through Consortium. Each year a distinguished poet is chosen to judge the prize and write an introduction to the winning book. The purpose of the prize is to encourage excellence in poetry, and to provide a wide readership for a deserving first book of poems. *The Reformation* is the sixteenth book in the series.

WINNERS OF THE AMERICAN POETRY REVIEW/
HONICKMAN FIRST BOOK PRIZE

The Reformation

Katherine Bode-Lang 9/20/14

Kalamazoo, Michigan

Katherine Bode-Lang

The Reformation

The American Poetry Review
Philadelphia

Cover art: *Pins* by Meridith Ridl.

Book design and composition: VJB/Scribe

Distribution by Copper Canyon Press/Consortium.

Library of Congress Control Number:
ISBN 978-0-97189-819-6 (pbk., alk. paper)

9 8 7 6 5 4 3 2 FIRST EDITION

ACKNOWLEDGEMENTS

A selection of these poems was previously published as a chapbook, *Spring Melt*, which was chosen by G.C. Waldrep as the second-place winner of the 2008 Keystone Chapbook Prize and was published by Seven Kitchens Press in 2009.

Grateful acknowledgment is made to the publications in which these poems first appeared:

American Poetry Review: "Beauty's Many Absences," "Morning Has Broken," "Notes on the Unseen," "Sanctuary"

Beloit Poetry Journal: "She's Heard It Said if It Weren't for the Sky We Would Go Mad"

The Cincinnati Review: "Christmas on the Coast," "Death in Midsummer," "Rainy Season"

Crab Orchard Review: "Watching the Front Move In"

The Greensboro Review: "September in the East"

Hayden's Ferry Review: "Daughter," "My Parents Getting Off the Plane in Guam, 1972"

Mid-American Review: "Lament for Pluto," "When the Weather Fails Us"

Nimrod: "In Drought, In Rain," "My Father's Fastball,"

Rattle: "Spring Melt"

Subtropics: "Daughter II," "Threshing"

The Sycamore Review: "Sorting the Socks of the Dead"

Third Coast: "The Pomegranate"

Toad the Journal: "The Dying of the Bees," "Mending," "Olbers' Paradox"

Tupelo Quarterly: "A Poem on Love," "Autumn Storm," "How Far We'll Go," "The Names of Snow," "The Reformation," "Translation," "When I Miss Paris Most," "When the Angels Go Bowling"

Thank you to Julia Spicher Kasdorf and Robin Becker for helping this book along in its early stages. Thanks also to my first poetry teacher, Jack Ridl, for giving us all joy in words. Many thanks to Laura Donnelly for her kind and careful reading

of this book at its turning point. I'm grateful to Elizabeth Scanlon for shepherd-
ing this book into the world and to Stephen Dunn for seeing the heart of 544.
Thank you to Valerie Brewster and Mimi for lending their eyes and their art to
this project. I appreciate the support of my colleagues, family, and friends—
especially Laura, Rebecca, and my sister, Libby.

Kim, you knew the spirit of these poems before I did but helped me find it on my
own—thank you.

Finally, my constant love and gratitude to Andrew, my best reader, my fiercest
believer, my sky.

NOTE

The title "Beauty's Many Absences" is from Alain de Botton's *The Architecture
of Happiness.*

for Andrew

Contents

Introduction

There were many fine manuscripts submitted to The American Poetry
Review/Honickman First Book Prize competition, and I finally found
myself going back and forth between three or four. But the one that
kept insisting on itself was number 544 (none of them contained the
name of the author), called *The Reformation*. "Insisting on itself," in this
instance, needs some explanation. One of the classic tricks of actors,
for example, is when you want to get the attention of your audience,
you lower, not raise, your voice. Katherine Bode-Lang's work is not a
trick, but the lowered voice kept attracting me to it in similar ways.
Whereas others would employ sensational langauge to convey impor-
tant or sensational moments, her work's power resided in its resis-
tance to melodrama, in its precise and often delicate phrasing.

    In "Olber's Paradox," a poem in which early on the speaker claims
"Everything falls apart/when I look up," she imagines this wasn't
true for Poe who "imagined the big bang of it all."

> Yet I like to hope that when
> he shut his lids, he could not see endless
> expansion, could not feel the axis tip
> and spin. Perhaps, like me, he only felt
> certain of night, the galaxy's eventual collapse,
> the moon coming in, then out, of our shadow.

This poem is typical of Bode-Lang's thoughtful, clear-minded com-
plexity, and the way her poems remain in dialogue with themselves.
She seems perpetually in search of what she feels and thinks, and,
without fanfare, finds it more often than not.

    Such searching is fundamental to the ongoing themes, which
are primarily suggested in the book's title. Throughout, we sense

the speaker trying to find ways to resist her family's staunch religiosity. She is, literally, a protestant who notices everything that might keep her from living a fuller life. Her reformation is part rebellion, and part a pursuit of remembering the value of what she's rebelling against.

> Wanting everything to survive,
> I know by instinct what to sacrifice.
> All day my hands smell of remembrance.

> "Pruning"

But nothing gets prettied up. In the exquisite title poem, which is as much a love poem to her husband as it is a statement of personal integrity directed to her parents, she acknowledges a malady she has. It's the second poem in the book, and it informs many of the poems that follow.

> Hear how this is, Mother? How my body pulled itself
> into the loudest *no*—the only part of me that knew
> how? Hear how this is, Father?...

> Do you see, Father, how he stayed?
> Look, Mother—he stayed.

> They do not know how you hold me as a teacup,
> how you are so gentle as you sip the porcelain rim.

> "The Reformation"

An even greater tough mindedness is exhibited in "Morning Has Broken," when she says, referring to the poem's title, "I always meant broken like the dishes." The poem goes on to lament that in her father's organ playing "there were no porcelain chips, just praise and elation," and concludes:

Don't believe what they tell you now:
morning was always breaking then,
and all the glass was stained.

"Morning Has Broken"

Nothing in *The Reformation* is forced or hyped. Her metaphors seem to arise naturally out of the working of situation and subject matter. No matter how personal, the poems don't feel confessional. She never forgets that she's writing poetry; her allegiance is to phrasing and sonics, and to the discoveries that occur from the management of those qualities. These virtues of hers promise a future. In the meantime, we have this fine first book.

Stephen Dunn

The Reformation

The Dying of the Bees

Lake Michigan, 2006

We expect carp and alewives,
slack and rotting along the shore.
Surely shells, inhabitants long wrung out.
But here, belly-up, are bees.

Not starfish, nor crabs, not beached
and heaving whales: we cannot
throw their landlocked bodies back.
The bees are restless as they die; we walk

cautious of their up-aimed barbs.
It's June, and later we'll call this
a long summer; how we counted
the wooden stairs up the dune

once waves took the bees—no one
ever did know why the sudden storm
of dying, not even the man
who walked the stairs each dusk, hammer
in hand, pounding back errant nails.

The Reformation

Vulvar Vestibulitis Syndrome, a subset of vulvodynia:

"chronic vulval discomfort characterized by burning, stinging, irritation and rawness of the vulva, or exquisite tenderness to touch on the vulval area or attempted vaginal entry"[1]

"...of unknown etiology and course with no agreed upon treatment"[2]

When my mother asks, tell her the fucking is fine.
Eight years, and we still have to love the tender parts of me
like a colicky baby.

No babies, though. None of the rollicking
that would make them. Just you.
You writing down the results of the culture this time.
You there every month when I open my legs
for the doctor's needles, swabs.

No one knows how you do it: the long drive, the hand
holding, that awkward standing next to the nurse.
When I say no one, I mean my mother.
I mean my sister, who feared it would be hers too
until the first boy. My father imagining my V spelled wife.

No sex.
They wonder why you stayed.
My mother, who could not hold my father

1. Wylie, K., Hallam-Jones, R., Coan, A., & Harrington, C. (1999). A review of the psycho-phenomenological aspects of vulval pain. *Sexual and Marital Therapy*, 14, 151–164.
2. Goldstein, A.T., Marinoff, S.C., & Haefner, H.K. (2005). Vulvodynia: Strategies for treatment. *Clinical Obstetrics and Gynecology*, 48 (4), 769–785.

without it. My father who returned to her only for dinner,
her long hair.

Those of us raised under the hand of Calvin,
we have been taught: lovemaking will break us against
our lover, fix us to each other anew. Come to the Midwest:
there are thousands of girls, blond ponytails, waiting.

Waiting because we have been told. Waiting because
we have not touched ourselves. Waiting because
he might not stay. Waiting for the aisle, the lifting
of the veil when we can finally call his name.

Those of us who are the eldest,
who knew no better, whose cheeks stung with sin,
we never expected it to hurt.
You and I never expected red and swollen. Never expected
it would stay past the vows, the first night.

Hear how this is, Mother? How my body pulled itself
into the loudest *no*—the only part of me that knew
how? Hear how this is, Father?

Mother, all my windows are broken. Father, I have crossed
my legs raw. But do you see, Father, how he stayed?
Look, Mother—he stayed.

They do not know how you hold me as a teacup,
how you are so gentle as you sip the porcelain rim.

She's Heard It Said if It Weren't for the Sky We Would Go Mad

This will be the blue rip that lets you see the moons of Jupiter with clarity,
the light ringing Saturn, our small planet seeking heat—this system spinning 30,000
       light-years
from the center of the Milky Way, a trillion stars in its spiral arms.

    Her mother writes: I fear the gray bowl about us,
    the wooden spoon you put to it. You have such clear eyes—
    you see the halos of the sun, its drifting, flaming spots.
    I want you to let the Black-Eye Galaxy go.

This will be the tear to show you the galaxy spanning light-years, how many
galaxies just like it hover close with gravity to our hive of stars;
this will shoot you past Andromeda and into the Virgo supercluster.

    Let skin be as hollow and as dark as the barrel
    of your telescope. Stop polishing lenses, cutting mirrors,
    seeing yourself as the Ocean of Storms. A girl
    cannot be the moon.

Cover a piece of sky with your thumb and the swirls of your skin hide
just one star. This will be the stone through the window that gives you galaxies like sand.
Where there is one star, there are shadows of a thousand galaxies. Your thumbnail
will fill with points of light. You will see galaxies of galaxies. You will want to cut your
       ear off.

    We can see 3,000 stars above the horizon on a good night.
    We can name the craters of the moon. We can calculate
    the distance to Delphinus. Do not forget the call
    of gravity. Do not draw constellations from his back.
    No longer be a burning point.

Diagnosis

All through my nap the woman one house over
chops vegetables in her kitchen. The clunk of the knife
on the cutting board, the uneven board

tipping on the counter tiles, the sink water running
over peppers—all of it echoes through one open window
to the next, sidles across the alley lined with garbage cans.

This and the clock tower mark my sleep and waking
in the afternoon; my fingers curl into fists when I dream,
unknot only when I wake, rise, look at my hands.

I imagine how windows shut for winter cut the air, the noise
of our days leaking like a wound. But it's early September,
we leave our windows open: the woman cooks,

a neighbor showers, another plays guitar.
Each window is a gaping mouth without a tongue,
our noises rumbling up from deeper down.

My Parents Getting Off the Plane in Guam, 1972

In the background: oil tankers, an orange
cargo vessel, the receiving factory
just beyond the twist of my mother's hair.

Countries have fallen, and they have flowers
on their heads, a camera looped around
my father's arm. Her smile will catch

you first—my father is just saying
something funny, eyes blinking, teeth showing
as he opens his mouth to laugh. She, in blue,

is leaning ever so slightly to him,
halfway around the world to work as the ocean
washes up boat after boat of refugees—

you wouldn't know it from the rise of her neck,
her lips parted slightly, her dark eyes following
the sound of low water. On this island

the grass yellows, and the heat is so new,
so strange, they will never understand
the thickness of the air. What we can't see:

her crying the first six months, black-haired
orphans, dark bottles of beer, rolls of confiscated film.
This picture—the only love story of theirs I know.

Daughter

I am my mother's pier
on a windy afternoon.
I am a broken necklace clasp,
a brown dress that no longer fits;

I am the braids her mother cut
off at the ears, kept in tissue
still plaited and bowed.
I am all my mother's *no's*.

I am my mother's straight chair,
her father's face. I am
her first cigarette, her last boy.
I am my mother's quiet.

I am my mother's shoulders,
the piano she never learned
to play, her little sister stillborn.
I am her last view of the lake.

When she holds my face,
it is her mother's sigh.

Note to My Cervix

You gave me a scare last week:
bled and bled on the doctor's table—
embarrassment first, fear a greater second.
All the babies I've never wanted
enter, exit quickly as imagined ghosts,
sheer as the examining sheet. Diagnosis made,
antibiotics begin traveling fast,
cells go quiet, heal. But all the small
openings for death still whisper in my body.
I have never thought of you before.
But now I imagine you: tucked in,
crimson as the leaves collapsing
this autumn, maples fierce and fading.

October Evening

One wish: to die in winter
when the cold first snaps
the branches and the pulp
of dormancy is nearly white.

To have made it through
one more autumn;
the trees' tail feathers
fanned, then dropped.

Just this—the smell of wood smoke,
fields fading yellow,
roadside sumac flaming
red to brown. On the front steps

November's mums surviving
me through the first snow.

Olbers' Paradox

> Were the succession of stars endless,
> then the background of the sky would
> present us an uniform luminosity
>
> EDGAR ALLAN POE, "EUREKA" (1848)

I can hardly handle the stars. Too many
little suns when the galaxy spins out
into arms, brushing against the bodies
of other galaxies just as bright.
Everything falls apart
when I look up. But not for Poe.
The paradox is simple: the sky

should glow. With all those stars, how is there ever
any night? Imagine him looking up,
realizing his eyes—careful
as they measure light—do not shrink,
do not narrow the pupils to a point. No,
instead this: dilation, opening, eyes rounding out
in recognition. His irises collect the dark
that shouldn't be. Before theories and redshift,
before Hubble, he imagined the bang of it all.

Yet I like to hope that when
he shut his lids, he could not see endless
expansion, could not feel the axis tip
or spin. Perhaps, like me, he only felt
certain of night, the galaxy's eventual collapse,
the moon coming in, then out, of our shadow.

End of Summer

The peaches, tired and bruised,
sit dying on the counter.
The shoulders of the tomatoes
split and sink, spoil on the sill.
We cannot keep up: limp beans,
wrinkled squash, red juicing berries.
Our waste.

How we'll wish for it
this February, months before
the first bitter lettuce seeds
push upward. My grandmother—
tired and confused now, bossy—
would cut, boil, save all August.
Even when she doesn't know
my age, her own age, she clucks in my head

at the careless kitchen.
Grandmother sits now with empty hands,
no crocheting, no crosswords,
just remembering dresses
she never owned, forgetting
phone calls she's already made.
On my answering machine: *I don't know*

where you are, please write me, tell me where you are.
I listen, throw food away, imagine
my grandfather out in the garden,
the back field already sold. How he tugs

at the dead roots, cannot hear
her dial the phone.

I cut this red pepper. A quick slice
opens into dark mold
nuzzling the seeds; black rot tearing
into the watery cells like winter. I sigh,
cut, eat. He weeds, gathers,
sits her down. Cut, save, again.

September in the East

All day this rain—you somewhere in a wool sweater.
Elsewhere, the sun a flattened penny in the sky,
hot as iron tracks just after the train.

The full harvest moon tonight, enough to light
the fields even after sunset; but we won't
see it—the valley rises and sinks with fog.

I do not miss the desert.
Except, perhaps, when I pull on my boots,
one of your shirts, and go walking. Past the creek

stretching out of its banks, over the path sticky
with wet maple leaves, I think I smell creosote,
the faint headiness like damp earth those little leaves release

only in rain. The only smell I now miss, so thick
in the summer heat when the storms finally broke,
we came to think of it as water.

Beauty's Many Absences

I stare at the wood showing beneath paint
chipped from the doorframe, so many layers of lead.

The man who nailed this together—
the wood that meets the door, the ceiling—is long dead.

Here, where the town sinks slowly with age,
we walk with the shadows of carriages and match factories,

cobblestones and lime quarries. We cannot possibly keep knowing,
keep breathing the dust of the dead who came before.

We must forget how the light, when it reaches us
from some distant star, has already gone brown with wanting.

Autumn Storm

Only mid-October, so the trees—still bright
with leaves—crack with the surprise of snow.

Cold splits the small elms at the tops of their trunks,
opens their branches like fingers pulling back corn silk,

tearing everything down with ice. Such destruction:
the broken branches, their red leaves, all bow low.

Second Note to My Cervix

Winter comes in fast and wet,
pulls the last leaves down
into the cold, and you,
with your red, wool sweater—
scratching *precancerous cells*—
have decided to stay the winter.
Outside, it's a snowstorm of white
pills and prescriptions all blowing
into nauseating drifts. I'd like to invite you

to hunker in, welcome you
like my mother, reheating
a pot of chili on the stove.
But we haven't made up
the guest room. If you stay
the season, we're going to need
more wood, more candles, extra blankets.
I'll shovel the drive, salt the walk.
There's sure to be ice
pulling at the gutters.
Don't walk under the eaves.

The Pomegranate

Had I known as a child what it was—what
the beveled seeds tasted like, blooming
inside the pulp of yellow insulation—I might
have understood Persephone.
Sister Emma's autumn of Greek lessons
never made sense—especially that story.
All those months away from Mother
for a fruit? But then, thick in the Midwest winters,
I had never tasted the tart stain.
Now further north, mid-December, we walk
among the dead, and I would still stay
for six sweet seeds bursting red
like small hearts in my mouth.

Sledding in the Cemetery

The graves ride the hills in the center of town, and with this much snow
no one clears the roads dividing plots by religion, date. So children gather, toss
themselves, fly, and then slow in the gravel kicked up from the plow's last run.

The granite headstones lift their smooth foreheads up out of the drifts. Our Dead
look on, smiling. Why wouldn't they? Imagining one more run down the slope,
belly on metal runners, bumps and icy dips rattling against the ribs, snow

catching and melting in the socks' ankles. Remembering how wind freezes the face,
the town's quiet are children again. It's not their houses, not hot mugs,
not their mothers warm and waiting—it's the cold they never meant to forget, or miss.

Sanctuary

My father and I sit before the sermons
in his study in the Texas apartment.

I am 23, he is 57; my parents are Midwest exiles
and there is no job after this church year—

just applications. My mother has taken to crying,
will not leave her room. So I sit with him,

cull through thirty years of funerals,
responsive readings. I know them all:

spent early mornings as a girl tucked in the hallway
outside his study, listening to him rehearse

to the empty house. Now I edit, photocopy,
organize the collections of his life for the churches in Utah,

Missouri, Washington—all places I am far from.
As a family, we have decided not to remember that winter,

but make no mistake: I chose the baptisms and the sermons too.
Stayed in that study until every file was sent.

It is my congregation.
But they do not know this:

with my absence and his blessing,
hands on the pulpit and hallelujah,

they are building a bigger sanctuary. Such glory.
And no one misses me. Not even him.

Threshing

February is a field, raspberry canes crooked and tied
with old sheets torn to strips. Warm enough that if
we hadn't just tucked you in like a tulip bulb,
you'd be out, considering when to plant the lettuce.

All of us wind-swept when they give your widow
the flag; black-suited pallbearers, the rain: it could be
a movie set. But here is the dirt, my father wearing
your ring, our open coats flapping. Now all the rooms

in the house are ripe tomatoes, and we are dull knives.
The farm will go with you, and later, we won't be here
to loosen the bows. With more rain, the fields flood
for spring; the season breaks down like a barn.

Snapshots

Here is the photo of the day my mother meant
to leave my father. Mother's Day, she wears an orchid;
I have just been christened—see the white dress.

Today is a month since my grandfather's funeral;
his widow wore an orchid too, just as she did every holiday.
After the burial, we packed her things and in the sewing closest

found the war photos, long hidden: her in a bathtub in San Francisco,
laughing. They were married two days before he shipped out.
But we did not take the letters from their string, did not read them:

one for every day, the thin pieces of paper that for three years
sailed their marriage back and forth across the Pacific.
All those years, before my father, the farm, 100-pound sacks of potatoes,

and this photo—when my mother did not leave. I am grown,
married when she tells me with a laugh how she had me in her arms
to walk out. But I was there the other times, saw the quiet leaving

of each parent: to the study, the kitchen, a sister's house.
Every time they came back, opened a door,
sat down for dinner. I did not fail to notice.

My Father's Fastball

Sometimes I like to imagine the other end
of one of my father's pitches—

not the backyard base-running of my childhood,
but the pitches when he was younger,

his four-seamer or slider, speed that would sting
when the ball hit your glove. Age 42, the fair's

pitching booth clocked him at 88;
he won a Pepsi t-shirt to prove it.

When I was older I learned about the contract
with the Pirates: the *no playing on Sunday* boy from Calvin College

turned it down. Went on to be a preacher,
coach; did pretty okay on the local teams.

I've always known my father with a scar on his knee.
When my husband turned 30, my father

mourned the passing as his own, said he'd known
he would never pitch that fast again.

It was all downhill from there.
The real prize at the fair was out-pitching

the younger guys. With his fastball at the top
of the carnie's chalkboard, my sister and I

had new teddy bears while our father—
for a night—remembered the mound,

the wind-up, the release when the ball left his hand.

Morning Has Broken

I always meant broken like the dishes;
though that's not what Cat Stevens—
or the hymn—meant. There were no
shards in the song when we danced to it,
the record scratched with skips.
No porcelain chips when my father
closed his eyes and listened to the organ,
just praise and elation in C major.
But that's what I was always thinking.
Don't believe what they tell you now:
morning was always breaking then,
and all the glass was stained.

How Far We'll Go

Three thin pricks
of the syringe along the cupped
curve of the vulva, and the red skin
breaks like a small dam.
I fainted—so Victorian, so
Freud's hysterical woman;
you'd have thought all the blood
in my body had escaped
through those small needle points.

Someone else might not have gone
pale, passed out; we never know
what will send us, drained and hazy.
One cracked tube of ammonia
under my nose, and I returned to cough
and complain. But even once
the gauze dried, once the nerves—
struck dumb—ceased their pulsing,
they would not let me stand.
Like bee stings the nurse had told me,
straight mouth, white gloves.

Translation

In Italian, *la passera* is *sparrow*,
a term of endearment
for the V tucked between my legs.
Il mio cielo—*my sky*, my lover.

My sparrow is a rainstorm,
is in a rainstorm, sheets of water and hail
airing on the wet street,
a question mark against the sky.
We count the seconds between lightning

and thunder. My lover calls
me *Bird*: a heron, a gull,
a sparrow—we have never
distinguished the species of bird,
nor the temperament of sky
when he calls my name.

My Husband Mourning

in memory of Maggie Wardle, 1980-1999

Her hands on his shoulders
this month. Her behind him
while he reads, turns the pages slowly.
He dreams: she walks the river
with him, smokes a cigarette.

Every night she wears a blue dress,
the one he likes to imagine she
wore inside the closed casket;
I held his left hand as he placed
his right palm on the polished wood

where her heart should've been.
Before sleep, down a hallway
seven years now, he hears another man's
shotgun loaded, cocked.

The first winter he made snow angels
in the grave's field. I watched him wish
for more snow, ice like a lighthouse.
I stood waiting on the other coast.

The Names of Snow

Of course we know how our language lacks:
it's a tangle of tenses and borrowed words, irregular
verbs and mixed constructions. Everything dangles
and we only have one word for love, a lament in itself,

echoed in every valentine. But think of all the other words
that hold up their hundred definitions: sky, wish, tree.
Or snow. There is sleet and freezing rain, hail
and "wintry mix," according to our Pennsylvania weatherman.

We lay adjectives before nouns like gifts, hoping
when we say them aloud we'll have made a new word,
when all we really want is more ways to say snow:
powder snow, flying snow, cotton snow.

As in Hokkaido, with such storms and so many names:
*a light sprinkling of snow, snow at the foot of a tree, beautiful morning
after a heavy snow*. Names for snow we've never seen:
one or two characters holding the world complete. As it is,

all the unknown words trail behind our thoughts, never
catching up. Still, I bless and keep my mother tongue,
even as I miss the words for everything that falls: night,
water, father. Perhaps it's not the words I miss

because I could just say "peony-flake snow."
But what if you did not know the heavy skirts
those flowers wear in early June?
Therein lies our sadness, the quiet in our mouths.

Sorting the Socks of the Dead

When they died, we wore their socks
on our hands for the winter. Puppets
with holes, our fingers poked out like ears.
Wool, white cotton, occasional stripes.
Nobody liked the faces of the socks
better than the faces of our dead.
It was a cold winter. The socks
murmured to each other, missed feet.
When we missed our friends, we would
drive, wave our hands out the windows,
the socks muttering like pigeons in a snowstorm.

On the Coast

Here's my mother, in love with ships.
The ferry docks hourly—she'll point it out,
the port appearing between bluffs and buildings.
When I visit, she drives me to the shipyard

where they repair fishing boats in winter:
cork the rotting hulls, replace warped wood,
strip the chipping paint. Daily she checks
on her boats (faded names, cracked masts),

drives to see the sailboats wet with varnish,
boats that reek of the Pacific. She talks to men
in dusty overalls who haul the ships out
on three-storey high hammocks, cranes with slings

that dip and rock the boats to shore.
Boats she knows: the salmon boat, the house boat,
Neil Young's yacht in for repair. My family owns no boats,
no docks, no clipped-grass lawn that ends at water.

In his study my father floats on a buoy of books.
Warm days they walk the pier. All week no one
mentions the rain. If there's a life boat
in this house, I don't know where it is.

Daughter II

I am my father's barn, the wall
he threw baseballs against all summer.
I am church twice on Sundays,
his mother's voice tight
around the kitchen table.

I am forty acres off the Benson woods
and candling eggs before school. I am
his correcting blue pen, his binoculars,
the poem he always wished he'd written.
I am my father's favorite hymn,
the pipe organ a half measure
after it splits the air.
I am not the first taste of raspberries.

I am hay bales and his first
Midwest winter. I am the scar on his knee
after he pitched the last game. I am not
the sign from God he'd asked for.
I am overgrown pepper plants and too much
shade. I am all rain and humidity,
a missing pair of scissors. Notice, Father,
how I have kept my hair long.

Rainy Season

Christmas Eve and the stacks of the paper mill slow for the evening,
    though the smell lingers stronger than salt or sea. Tanker ships
with their red metal containers float like rusted gifts through the straits.
    And we, like the trees, bend and snap against the season's short days.
The whole town is soaked: winter rains fill ditches, flood yards,
    blur the windows so next-door Christmas lights twinkle twice. Tomorrow,
we'll unwrap piles of paper, and then the factory will begin again—
    pump the grime of cardboard and pine across the saturated Sound in
gray, sour clouds. That smell again. The pulp won't dry till spring.

Waiting for the Church to Burn

I have been waiting so patiently.
Through sermons and prayers, hymns
and coffee hour, I have been waiting.

In pink dresses and shined shoes,
fixed smiles and choir robes,
I have been waiting. The buildings

of my childhood have come down one
by one: The barn went first, then the house
to the teeth of a bulldozer (the neighbor needed

a bigger yard). The school fell
under the bishop's heavy hand, and all
that's left to go is the church.

I have seen from this matchbox of a town
how bricks do not burn but bake and fall,
take roofs and windows with them.

Could fire fell a steeple? I'll wait.
I've learned just how much is possible
when the tinder is so dry.

That First February

It must have been so cold—or at least everything, everyone
dying made it seem like it might never thaw. You wrapped me in your
big shirts when I stayed the night: the concrete floor

so cold beneath the bed we nested our bodies all night.
You brought me daffodils, the miniature ones
with their sweet yellow lips whispering of warm air.

The only warmth was when we walked the river, and
you cupped your hands around your mouth to light a cigarette:
that momentary flame, the smoke to prove it, all the promises—

which we kept. You quit smoking years ago, and it is not nearly
so cold now. Every March, I buy daffodils at the grocery store.

Spring is lazy, but it always finds us. We did not know then
that it was possible for love to stay, even through
the winter, even when the roof buckles under ice.

The Second Year

From our apartment we can hear the car bumpers, rusty barrels, stove parts
falling and meeting in the industrial recycling yard—the magnet on the crane
as it pulls the tops off hills of long-indistinguishable metal. Barges on the channel,

already heavy with coal, wait for the next load of scrap metal, chain-link fencing.
All day they make their way up and down the channel to the lake, awaiting a
        new buoyancy
in Milwaukee, or later through the locks and into the Atlantic, waiting

for the disburden of iron and gravel, the rising of water. And as we lie here
on our blue sheets, I can feel my back, my shoulders lighten and lift,
the slow movement of our bodies all night through the channels, looking for open water.

Spring Melt

They separate in March:
the first of our friends

to decide on divorce.
We tiptoe around the month;

we've been fighting,
too. Our house is an

over-starched shirt.
The month is dark with rain,

the streets all slick
like sadness. We wait,

rarely patient, for a thaw,
for our hands to unknot

into hands again. But
our friends are an ice floe

breaking apart in spring's
thick current. We pull

the muck of winter
from the gutters, hope

the water will run clean again;
nothing more than this:

we hold onto each other
like an upturned boat—

even if cold can never
really go away, even if

we might always feel the frost
at the edges of our bodies.

Notes on the Unseen

The lady on the bus says she's sure the seasons fell off
rotation when the ocean rose into a wall—*tsunami*—
sank like a shipwreck with a country in it. In those thin seconds,
she tells us, the axis skipped; so March, mixed-up month,

dips in and out of winter, spring. Seasons, invisible
as ever, float like steam from my tea cup, like the shadow
of steam the sun casts on our table. Even the photos
flooding our morning newspapers never made visible

the noise of the wave, or the thoughts of the dead—all
that is lost with the camera lens and its glass translation.
Same with the captioned names: each name only a messenger,
the paper envelopes of men and women. I like to imagine our dead

smiling when they hear their names, though each has the same name
of a thousand others. I saw white gulls, unmarked envelopes
appearing over the snowy ground, only against the trees,
the dark sky, then descending, dying back into the white, the snow.

In the Back Field

Spring, and all thoughts of death return—
the tangled seeds and sprouts that won't grow
back where tar paper and bricks thicken

the rotted branches and leaves. The buzz of early
April heat in the air, but winter's wake is everywhere:
concrete collapsed to moss, iron pipes eroded,

shingles lifted from the shoulders of the barn.
And the fields, dormant until now, open
fiercely to the sun. We, winter-worn like the weeds,

will our skin to blush and singe, will anything
to send out green shoots. This small bug, better
with instinct, tucks its appendages in

with the approach of my breath. We are not so careful.
Every year cranes stop in France, returning from Africa,
and what we have wanted all along folds with the heat.

My mother timed her summer days by a bell
on the east side of the house—her mother calling
the children to return for dinner. No bell here,

but I walk back through bare bushes and recall the sound
of my mother's voice, the color of my grandmother's hair.
My skin catches against a new thorn and bleeds out winter's rust.

Letters From the 80th Year: A Found Poem

for Ann Woodin

Now about birthdays: forget about birthdays.
Oracle is proud of its oak trees, as some women
are proud of their hair. Six months without rain;
here are five dead oaks out my kitchen window.
This one still alive is watered by the leaking faucet.
Your letter opened my bag of memories:
in England, we had lunch with Daisy, a Duchess
(her sister married the last Raj of India); the boys
had perfect manners. Even the stern butler smiled at them.
In the desert the boys couldn't climb trees.
Tender-hearted Hugh watched *Moby Dick*—
he was so upset about the harpooned whales.
"Well, salt water is good for cuts," he said.

Without Nostalgia

At just the right light, the sun
finds the cardinal like it did the canyons
in the desert so that, momentarily,
this small red glow flits around the tree,
almost orange in the sunrise.

I am surprised that I might miss
the rock, how the cliffs would transform
in the light before falling back into heat.
As I watch, the sun shifts its way up

our own hills, and the tree is green again,
and I am returned here to this side of the country,
this morning where you are in the kitchen
waiting for the coffee to brew.

Watching the Front Move In

My jaw has taken on the stubborn, taut complaint
of a too-tight hinge. Only the doctor can hear
the nearly silent snip of bone, the click of resistance
between bone and cartilage, like the click of high heels

on the polished stone of the narthex.
I think of stained glass windows, the organ,
the church I have not been to for years:
where I was married, where everyone was buried,

where my father held the marble pulpit with both hands,
gesturing into the dark Sunday. I think of all the people
I have not seen since then, a congregation gathered
around our dinner table every night. None of this I miss.

Though there was the music. How it produced such faith—
we swelled with belief when the choir opened their mouths,
the cathedral swallowing our thousand voices.
My jaw still catches when I open it; I pray sound comes this time.

Dear Grandmother

I am told you are dying, and
I will think of you tonight. Here,
a front is moving in, and the lightning
bugs spark before the thunder.
It is hot, and everything sticks:
the windows, our clothes, this sadness.
The final slowing of your breath
has been expected, but now,
imagining it is your last night, everything
seems sudden—the sky, the storm,
its passing. As you die tonight,
dear grandmother, I will stay
this storm and think of you.

Think of you watching baseball games
on television and believing you were
there. Think of you warning my sister
about marrying a carpenter—so many
cupboards. Think of the letters you sent me,
your handwriting slanting ever down
the page, sparkling stickers on the envelopes
when I was far past twelve. The last letter
you wrote *My writing is really terrible*
because it really isn't my writing.
And so I think you've known.

When you'd forgotten how to walk,
forgotten where you lived, forgotten
whole decades, you remembered
death, the instinct that never leaves,

that patiently waits. You've always known
what to do now: curl in, go someplace quiet.
It is like the weather that we can never
predict, yet we've been practicing all our lives.
And still, such terrible noise tonight,
grandmother, after all that light.

Family History

Most every glass of orange juice,
I think of my grandfather,
remember his stories of Christmas morning:
thirteen stockings, one orange in each.

Every morning I drink the guilt
of generation—my father picking
strawberries, age six, nickel a box.
He walked the lines of plants

with the other boys every day
but Sunday. Like my grandfather
and his brothers before the war,
their bodies stooped to the seasons;

the farmers worried school
wouldn't let out before the berries
blushed too heavy. With the burden of oranges
all these years, I have never imagined

my father might have stopped
to lift a perfect strawberry to his mouth,
the taste of red under his small tongue
like a communion wafer.

I have forgotten the fields behind the farm:
the hedges of blackberries that kept the cows;
rows of apple trees straight as soldiers;
raspberries all August. Not knowing

that every summer my father climbed
the backyard cherry tree, fought the birds
to eat. Not thinking to envy the dark berry stains
on my grandfather's tan, late-summer hands.

Never realizing what they'd gathered,
what always gets left behind.

Love Letters

In her last days, when my grandmother can no longer speak
or cry, my sister reads to her the love letters
my grandfather sent throughout the war.
This is why we believe in heaven—

because we want to believe that the sweet twine
that held the letters might also hold us
to each other and to the world.
That the silken threads of love survive
and pull us to the next life.

Why else should there be such fervor
in our prayers? Sometimes it's the trees or
a perfect glass of water that makes us want to stay.
And sometimes it's those letters
that make us wish we'd followed right away.

Death in Midsummer

Our roundness and constant spinning, our shift and tilt,
are imperceptible until the orange blade of the moon
sinks too quickly into the humid hills.

It slices the low mountains' veins so they bleed
mist from the rivers that first cut them. Soon fog
takes the sky to clouding, thick and starless now.

When the Angels Go Bowling

With every storm I am six again: thin panic
against a breaking sky.
I unplug everything from the walls,
bury myself in the bed as thunder cracks

at rooftops, rattles windows.
Lightning is never beautiful
nor fascinating; I cower from a sky
I do not control.

My father once told me,
You cannot stop a hurricane.
But how I tried with my mother:
smiling, pleading—certain

I could stop trees from snapping,
lightning from striking.
But when her front blew in, I was always
a jangle of downed wires and flooded streets.

All thunder tolls for me,
small and running barefoot
down the hall toward any open door.

Passing

In the letters he sent you during the war,
filed in a shoebox after your death,
there is a missing baby—

a miscarriage years before my father. No one is alive now
to know: all your sisters dead, and you had run
away to San Francisco anyhow.

We do not have your words, but your husband's—
one sentence of sadness imagining "Junior's"
first birthday. It seems there is so much

you took with you, and it's no surprise
none of us can find anything. You once told me
the single memory of your father:

how you walked in a field with him by yourself.
Fourteen children—you were alone with him
just once. Dear Grandmother,
I have always been alone with my father.

Pruning

I am pruning the herbs.
I do not actually know
how to do this. My husband
planted them, cuts lavender or thyme
for dinner, waters them between
rains. But here I am with fingernails
and kitchen shears, finding my way
through the tangle of scent to where
the spindly rosemary bolted off
a thick branch. I cut
at the crossroads of the woody stalk.

I think I'm helping the plants,
but I can't say for sure—haven't read
a book or looked this up.
Instead, I am young, watching
my grandmother hover
over her red geraniums.
Some mornings she spent
hours bending and trimming,
deadheading her porch's flowers.
Even passing by,
she always found something
waiting for her to reach down,
pinch off with her thumb and forefinger,
her well-filed nails snipping
stems at their start.

I know my father pruned
apple trees out front,
and my grandfather was always
pulling something from the garden.
So while I think this is instinct,
it's more likely practice
twenty years back and more,
summer tutoring I don't remember:
a line of family lessons lead to this morning,
when I am cutting out the dead,
even if I must take new growth
with it. Wanting everything to survive,
I know by instinct what to sacrifice.
All day my hands smell of remembrance.

When I Miss Paris Most

Once a month we drive there, drive home; I dress,
undress—four hours, one specialist, swabs, cultures.
The hope that this time my tiny cells and spores
will tell their secrets to a thin, glass slide. He holds
my hand while the doctor touches with a Q-tip,
the cotton-soft pain test: *Where does it hurt? One to three?*

Three's the worst. She runs her gloved fingers
around that familiar circle. And I wish she looked
as lovely as the woman we saw in Paris—
how alone at the café she leaned over her wine glass,
traced its thin edge, listening for the shine of sound.

In Drought, In Rain

Out buying your birthday gift I run into a friend, new
in love. He hasn't slept in days; the thought of the woman
wound so tightly around his chest he can barely breathe.

I am just buying you a book. I tell you this over dinner.
We eat, remember storms in the desert, when every surface
glowed with the electricity of the sky—dusty wind across the bed,

the morning wet and polished. Now the cat sleeps on our quiet bed,
her paws across the pillows. Our breathing is steady, patient. But here:
my arms reach over you like a tree bough, the light on the mountains.

No, I come to you in the morning as if you were a wheat field,
an orchard, and I am a bird who has been hungry all night.

A Poem on Love

for A.

When I first met him, it was the river,
frost on the windows in the morning, olive oil.
Then bread and wine, the mountains.
Coffee, comfortable chairs. Lights. When he loves,
he loves so fully, it's as if the world did not
exist for him before the sound of dried leaves
on the sidewalk or the moon quietly rising.
He has brought every small joy with him,
a tender trail marking the way to here: today,
late afternoon when the sky fills and the trees
start to scratch. Watch him marvel at the color gray.

Wedding Poem

for Matt and Mary

There are two chairs in a room,
you in yours, your lover in the other.
The air around you is a glass of water you share.
Imagine your hands, your lover's hands,

how they fold and wring, touch your spine,
the spines of books. You've always hoped
your life would pull itself taut against another's life.

There is no advice for marriage, save that you
share that water. Know the bonds of oxygen
and hydrogen will be enough, your own bodies
of water touching, keeping space between you.

You knew it the first time you held her
to your chest and felt the sound of water
like a shell, the world opening in the smallest of spaces.

Postcard from Star Island

The mail arrived to-day, but nothing for me.

NATHANIEL HAWTHORNE, *PASSAGES FROM
THE AMERICAN NOTE-BOOKS*

Today I am Nathaniel Hawthorne. I write on these rocks
near the cove, look across to Laighton's Hotel.
It's September 1852, and I am ten grateful miles
east of Portsmouth. The weather's warm,
and the fishing's poor. I watch the boats.
In my room there is a box of pears.

All morning I have been wondering about the birds,
small birds at night that dive at the lighthouse lantern
as if it were a sky, hit the shining glass but not the flame.
I am told I could collect a bushel of their bodies
at the lighthouse base should I stay the summer.

Fever

Two weeks till the end of school,
and everybody coughs and sniffles, hacks
and fevers as the forsythia opens in bright
yellow. The whole town swaps sneezes;
we pass colds and germs like it's a potluck.
There's no deadly strain of scratchy throat,
but still, I worry over my body as if it were a nest.

Worry because I've been reading about 1918,
how everyone young died. Worry
because all the magazines press the panic
button—*avian*, *epidemic*, *vaccine*.
Worry because everything inert could kill me:
my new fiberboard desk off-gassing formaldehyde,
the PVC shower curtain, unwashed vegetables.
I pay careful attention to my lungs,
wash and rewash my hands raw.

Can't you see? The tulips haven't made
their colored cups yet, the cherry's barely pink.
I couldn't leave now, not before the windows
are all open, before the hills blink wide
with leaves, not before it all comes back.
Let me leave in the thick of it.

Fuse

Uncle Chuck is dying in his only brother's living room,
a blue, loaned hospice bed by the back window.
The last weekly visit I remember, I'm sixteen;
he sits shirtless at the white kitchen table shooting dice,
the oxygen tank like a rocket launcher by his chair. It's July,

staples keep the cancered esophagus tucked away.
His breathing rattles like the dice—but all we hear:
the quiet click, click of the silver Zippo sparking
under his thumb. Click, click. A "do not resuscitate" sign
by the phone, the only parent *tsking*. We've heard the other aunts:

skirt-chaser, *cheat*; my sister and I do not compete
for our uncle with the red sports car and smuggled parrot,
a python and pinball machine, tattoos and fireworks
—the magic of what my parents call, hushing,
black market. We didn't ask questions; just waited

for his yearly arrival on the Harley, then
the pop of Black Cats and rows of Roman candles,
fizzing bottle rockets, deafening aerials.
He held the lighter to the fuses, the fierce
meeting of oxygen and spark, a click to light the sky.

Mending

I spent that summer tucked behind the library's stacks
with broken books, repairing bends and tatters,
erasing pencil marks, tipping in the missing pages.
Old books, weak and torn books, all came to my table—

covers like rags. I undressed them further: removed
battered cloth with cuts through the spine and name,
down inside joints still holding flapping limbs to well-stitched pages.
Once undone, I would fashion a cast—red, green, black, or blue—

cut cloth and bristol board, build a new spine,
fasten on the covers with a batch of glue I made that week.
The dressing so fitted, I would paint pages back together, layer tissue
over tears, splint the bent corners, slip waxed paper

under the eyelids of the book. In my windowless room,
a ward of old books lay quiet, pinned and drying
between bricks and boards. My handwriting later named them,
numbered and tagged them, sent them back to metal shelves.

Burden of Proof

No agreed upon treatment.

So it comes and goes, stays. Since the beginning,
I have believed I could think my way better.
Visualization, vitamins: it would be so simple.

When I told my parents, they sent me to therapy.
Which made it true: *it's all in my head.*
But I didn't get better. It didn't get better.

Even when it was pills and spore counts,
the medicine only worked a little, at times.
Because the body keeps what is wrong,

holds shame till it is amber,
a fossil calcified into staying, reminding.
I have thought I did not have the strength,

nor the will, nor the depth of spirit to
touch my own cloak and heal myself,
but it's my body that knew,

down to the folded pink fabric of my self,
how to watch the horizon, gauge the clouds.
Before they tell me again,

it's all in your head. Watch my body prove,
year after year, as long as it must:
it is not, it is not, it is not.

Marche Funèbre

Chopin's dirge, we hear it now only in movie funerals,
a student's sulk to the principal's office. It plods,
mutters *200 years old, rain*. The sonata, though, is unexpected,
a slow ascension to sad; the melody so hidden we say

it sounds like a tune we think we know. But here is what we've missed:
the high B-flat in the eleventh measure, third movement—
how it floats as the echo of the lowest note, boots in mud
five octaves above. It falls down the scale for just two measures,
then disappears, and history forgets. But that small chord,

literally minor, lifts the ribs, remembers movement, heaves the chest
into a sigh, a crack in the familiar music. What we didn't expect
but knew must have been there all along: Chopin's last glimpse of sky.

Lament for Pluto

Imagine all the teachers,
almost September, grumbling
as they remove the small blue
Styrofoam orb hanging from
the farthest wire of the mobile
brought out for science class.
Reclassified in Prague: *dwarf planet*.
Like the comet Ceres, a giant
among comets, but not quite
a planet. Same with 2003 UB313,
so small, so young, it still has no name.
You, at least in name, remain godlike.

For 76 years we counted you;
now Clyde Tombaugh sighs
in his grave. But maybe he already
knew: 1930, only 24, newly hired
at Lowell's Observatory—the first
American to ever find a planet.
But it was a losing battle,
poor Pluto, smaller than our moon.
How badly we wanted you.
Your removal from dioramas and diagrams
the oldest of eulogies, a name's
quiet resignation. You can't help
that your orbit competes

with a thousand other orbits
we have not named. We,
who have stood at the far

corner of the classroom, or down
the hallway, representing you
if the sun is this golf ball...
we will miss you. Elementary school
graduates of the last century
will still refer to *nine planets*
while our children tick off eight.
Such misunderstanding:
our solar system shrank,
though we are told
we are ever-expanding.

The Boys

Boys speed and skid
down the hill
in front of our house—
brakes off their bikes,
sneakers dragging asphalt.
The squeals of their wheels
and feet are familiar now.
We, less reckless, would never
heat the bottoms
of our feet with speed.
So we shake our heads
as they fly by each evening
and wonder: how do they
get to the top of the hill?
We never see them
struggle up. It's as if the world
each night keeps giving us
these boys: shaggy hair
and black t-shirts,
swearing and spitting,
the town's ragged edges
showing on their frayed cuffs
and bony arms.
They careen down,
detached from everything
but gravity, as if the wind
could carry them off
limb by shoe by hat.
Who would notice if
they flew off the road tonight?

With nothing holding them,
not even their crying shoes,
they fly down, night after
night—one long plea
that the world let go this time.

When the Weather Fails Us

I.

August, and every afternoon now
clouds come up over the Catalinas,
humid and dark as mold clinging
to the rubber strip inside the refrigerator door.

The pigeons wait for the rain
with inelegant patience, bob on
a rainbow between utility poles,
color rising from the shimmer of wires.

Before the rain, all doubt rushes in
like an ocotillo thorn catching
against a bare shoulder. And I wonder,
what about the last page?

Will I simply stop one day?
Or will death take me? And a dear one
will find the last poem and think:
here she was this morning.

As when I was the dear one, and drove the car home
from the gym after his heart attack. Turned the key
and the CD clicked in: Coltrane, mid-song.
We grow so sad at times our skin is a tarp

slapping against itself in the storm.

II.

Think of everything as a potential flood plain.
Vision like the dam builders.

The first drop hits the roof. I will
turn off the fan so you can hear it better.
The chimes over the concrete patio
rattle themselves. And now the smell.
The ground is only briefly wet, the concrete

like sauna rocks, but the dirt
cracks to mud momentarily.
The smell: creosote with its tiny quick
green leaves of scent. The thunder
reverses on itself with sound.
This morning in the paper: a boy,
a high school football player, was attacked
by a black bear in Connecticut.
The boy punched the bear in the chest
and ran. He is left
with only welts and a good story.
Should I find myself in Connecticut,
I'll know what to do.

III.

The homeless woman of the neighborhood
walks by with her grocery cart of cans.
She stops at our green garbage barrel, looks in,
walks on. The broken wheel of the cart
announces its hobble far down the street.

The rain stopped with the bear story.
What do I tell you now?
Some days, it is as simple as what we long for
in the morning when we first wake—

we have thought of nothing else
all night long. Everything quiet and angry
comes to us in the night, and in the morning
there is more rain, the expansion of our lungs

with air, breath moving back into the world,
the movement of dust on the screen,
the screen to the sky, the lock you will undo
to let out the air, let in the air, that compromise.

About the Author

Katherine Bode-Lang was born and raised in western Michigan. Her chapbook, *Spring Melt* (Seven Kitchens Press), placed second in the 2008 Keystone Chapbook Contest and earned the New England Poetry Club's Jean Pedrick Chapbook Award. She has published in numerous journals, including *The American Poetry Review*, *The Cincinnati Review*, *Tupelo Quarterly*, and *Subtropics*. Katherine earned her MFA in poetry at Penn State University, where she is now an IT Trainer in the Office of Research Protections. She lives in central Pennsylvania with her husband, Andrew.